Old Dad Cunn

story by Keith Gardner
pictures by David Williams

Old Dad Cunningham still had his dogs.

People laughed at him.
Once they had needed dogs to go up country in the snow.
Now they had helicopters and there was little work for the old man and his dogs.

But when the snow came he took his dogs out …
just to let people see what he did.

"Why do you keep your dogs?" people asked Dad.
Old Dad would give them a funny look.

"I like dogs," he would say.
"They are my friends, and there may come a time when we need our friends."

Then some very bad snow came. People could not get out, and in the hill country there was very little for the animals to eat.

When the helicopters could take off, they went out to help.

Still the snow came.
A man on the radio said that it would keep on coming.

Then, one morning, it was so bad that the helicopters could not take off.

At the helicopter station they had to think about what they could do.

One man said, "We have got to get to Red Pine. We said we would fly Tom Parker out this morning. If we don't do it..."
He stopped.
Tom Parker was in a very bad way.

"What about a snow car?" another man asked.

"No way," the first man said.
"Red Pine is in the hill country.
A snow car would never get there."

"I can get to Red Pine," said Old Dad Cunningham.
They all looked at him.

"I'll get to Red Pine," he said again.
"The dogs will get me there –
and back again."

Once, the men had laughed at Old Dad Cunningham, but they did not laugh now.
He was the one man who could get Tom Parker out of Red Pine.
"You know what you are going into," they said.

"I know the hill country, and I know all about how to get there in bad snow," said Dad.

Old Dad Cunningham set off with his dogs.

He talked to the dogs all the time, as they ran across the snow.

"Come on, Skip...! Come on, Ben! Wait, Lad... wait! Ho... Ho... Ho... up, Jet."

Skip was the old dog and went first.
All the time, his eyes were looking
here and there.
The snow hid the tracks to the hill country,
but Skip found a way.

On and on they went.

At last, as night came, they got to
Red Pine. Tom Parker was very, very bad.
"You will have to wait for morning,"
said Kay Parker.

"No," said Dad Cunningham.
"We'll get Tom back as quick as we can.
Come on, men, feed the dogs for me, and
some of you can help with Tom."

The dogs had some food and a rest, then they set off again into the night.
Now there was danger round about them all the time.

"Home, Skip,"
Dad called out in a gruff sort of way.
"I know you are tired, old boy,
but we can do it."

Without Skip they would have been lost.
When the snow and the night hid the tracks
and the signs that Dad could follow,
Skip never stopped.
He was going home.

Old Dad was so tired, he was like a
man walking in his sleep.

First thing in the morning they got back.
People ran to Old Dad Cunningham,
"You did it, Dad! You did it!" they shouted.

"The dogs did it . . . not me," said Dad.
"You see to Tom.
I want to see to my dogs."

Tom Parker was soon up and about again, and he went back to Red Pine by helicopter.

Now people never laugh at Old Dad Cunningham. They think about a time when they will need the dogs again.